21st Century
Junior Library

INFOGRAPHICS: ENGINEERING A WIN

Sports-Graphics Jr.

Stephanie Loureiro

Published in the United States of America by:

CHERRY LAKE PRESS
2395 South Huron Parkway, Suite 200, Ann Arbor, Michigan 48104
www.cherrylakepress.com

Reading Adviser: Beth Walker Gambro, MS, Ed., Reading Consultant, Yorkville, IL

Photo Credits: © Gino Santa Maria/Shutterstock, © tharrison/Getty Images, © RobinOlimb Getty Images, © JuliarStudio/Getty Images, © checha/Getty Images, cover; © Jessica Orozco, 7; © Jessica Orozco, 8; © Jessica Orozco, © drvector/Shutterstock, 9; © Victoria Sergeeva, 10; © pikepicture/Shutterstock, 11; © lioputra/Getty Images, © lioputra/Getty Images, © Michal Sanca/Shutterstock, 12; © bor-zebra/Getty Images, 14; © Jessica Orozco, 19; © Jessica Orozco, 20; © Jessica Orozco, 21

Cherry Lake Press is an imprint of Cherry Lake Publishing Group.

Library of Congress Cataloging-in-Publication Data has been filed and is available at catalog.loc.gov.

Cherry Lake Publishing Group would like to acknowledge the work of the Partnership for 21st Century Learning, a Network of Battelle for Kids. Please visit Battelle for Kids online for more information.

Printed in the United States of America

Note from publisher: Websites change regularly, and their future contents are outside of our control. Supervise children when conducting any recommended online searches for extended learning opportunities.

ABOUT THE AUTHOR

Stephanie Loureiro is a writer and editor. She's been writing since she was nine years old and loves working on books that help kids discover things they love. When she's not writing, she can be found curled up reading a book, doing Olympic weightlifting, or singing loudly and dancing around to Taylor Swift. She currently lives in Idaho with her husband, daughter, and two dogs.

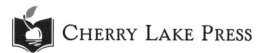

CHERRY LAKE PRESS

CONTENTS

BETTER TECH, BETTER PERFORMANCE

Many competitive sports have been around for hundreds of years. Technology has made sports even better. It has helped athletes perform better. Athletes now have better uniforms and equipment. They also have new and better ways of training. These changes are thanks to **engineering.** Engineering is solving problems by using science and math.

TIMELINE OF SPORTS TECH

1990: TITANIUM CLUBS
Titanium is a type of lightweight metal. In 1990, special golf clubs called drivers were first made of titanium. Titanium driver clubs allow for more control. Golfers have a faster swing, too.

2012: NEW HELMETS
Concussion helmets reduce the chances of players getting concussions if they are hit by a ball. The 2012 upgrade works against ball speeds up to 100 miles (161 kilometers) per hour.

1954: SHOT CLOCK
The National Basketball Association (NBA) introduces the 24-second **shot clock.** There is a swift increase of 14 points per game (PPG). More scoring makes games more exciting.

2008: LZR SWIMSUIT
The Speedo LZR Racer suit is made of high-tech fabric. It reduces **drag** and water resistance. It was banned 2 years later from the Olympic Games because it helps swimmers too much.

2013, Complex

ENGINEERED EQUIPMENT

Technology in sports may seem like a new idea. But it has been a part of sports since the 1920s.

Players and teams want the best tech. It helps them play better. This drives new **innovations.** Video technology is one of these. Virtual imaging is another. There are even new devices that track time to help athletes. All of this engineering can lead to more wins!

BASEBALL SPECS

DIAMETER
2.86 to 2.94 inches
(7.3–7.5 cm)

LACES THICKNESS
0.1875 inches
(0.4763 cm)

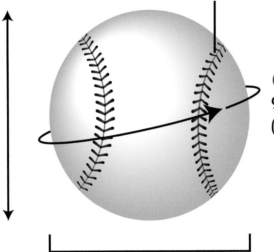

CIRCUMFERENCE
9 to 9.25 inches
(23–23.5 cm)

WEIGHT
5 to 5.25 ounces (141.7–148.8 grams)

FOOTBALL HELMET HISTORY

In some sports, there is a high risk for injuries. Football players are often tackled. Players need to be protected. That way, they can keep playing—and keep winning! Football helmets have seen many changes over the past 100 years.

Hard leather helmets have straps that keep the skull away from the helmet shell.

The NFL makes helmets required.

1920s

1930s

1943

1940s

1950s

1953

1955

1960s

1962

Plastic helmets become widespread.

Soft leather helmets are used.

Chin straps are used, there are graphics on helmets, and the NFL makes an official move to plastic helmets.

Face masks change to double bar.

The first face mask (single bar) is used.

The first helmet with a radio is created so players and coaches can talk.

The NFL requires face masks.

"Revolution helmets" reduce concussions.

1970s

1980s

1990s

2000s

2010s to present

Lightweight polycarbonate helmets cushion blows.

The air bladder system absorbs more impact.

Face mask grills become popular.

The NFL continually looks for ways to protect **league** players as well as future generations.

BETTER BODIES

Today, athletes can run faster and jump higher. They throw faster and hit harder. Why? New info has helped coaches and athletes. They know how to train and play better. And medical experts take better care of them, too. Nutrition is one example. Experts have shown that nutrition plays a key role in fueling athletes.

NUTRITION NEEDS OF A BASKETBALL PLAYER

PROTEIN

0.6 to 0.8 grams per pound of bodyweight (1.4–1.7 grams/ kilograms of bodyweight)

CARBOHYDRATES

2 to 4.5 grams per pound of bodyweight (4.4–10 g/kg bodyweight) 55% of total daily **calories**

FATS

Remaining daily calories

TOMMY JOHN SURGERY

Tommy John surgery is one of the most common surgeries for athletes. It fixes damage to pitchers' elbows.

90% success rate of Tommy John surgery	82% of MLB pitchers return to the league after surgery	15% of patients experience tears again

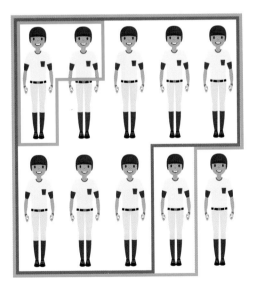

2013, American Journal of Sports Medicine

GETTING STRONGER, THROWING HARDER

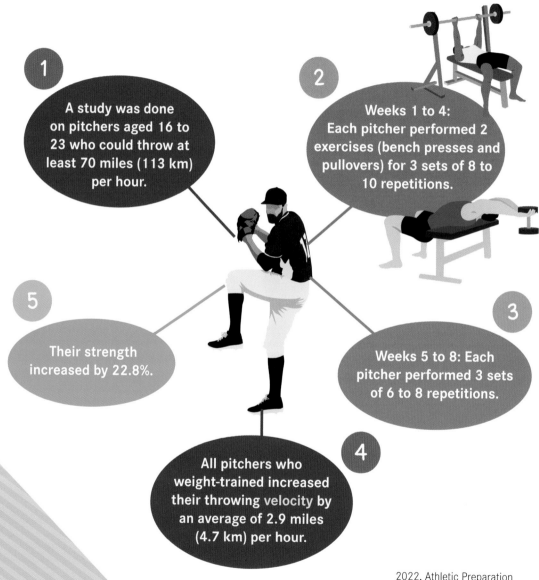

1 A study was done on pitchers aged 16 to 23 who could throw at least 70 miles (113 km) per hour.

2 Weeks 1 to 4: Each pitcher performed 2 exercises (bench presses and pullovers) for 3 sets of 8 to 10 repetitions.

3 Weeks 5 to 8: Each pitcher performed 3 sets of 6 to 8 repetitions.

4 All pitchers who weight-trained increased their throwing velocity by an average of 2.9 miles (4.7 km) per hour.

5 Their strength increased by 22.8%.

2022, Athletic Preparation

ENGINEERED ENVIRONMENTS

There are many things that can affect how well athletes play. Some are ones that we might not even think of. Engineers and mathematicians have studied field surface. They study the **acoustics** of stadiums. They even study air temperature. They want to know how these things impact game play. Some things can help athlete performance a lot. But some things don't. Not all sports engineering leads to more wins.

THE ICE STANDARD

The first indoor hockey game was in Canada in 1875. The rink was made of a sheet of ice. It was 85 feet (26 meters) wide and 200 feet (61 m) long. The 1875 ice remains the standard for National Hockey League (NHL) rinks!

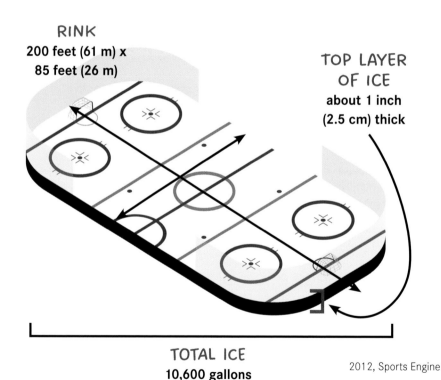

RINK
200 feet (61 m) x
85 feet (26 m)

TOP LAYER
OF ICE
about 1 inch
(2.5 cm) thick

TOTAL ICE
10,600 gallons
(40,125 liters) of water

2012, Sports Engine

WONDERS OF ENGINEERING

Breaking records is a hard thing to do. But athletes have better chances of doing so now. They have the help of newer equipment. They have better training programs. And they can wear special gear. Some innovations even help too much. They might create an unfair advantage.

A RECORD-SETTING OLYMPICS

Many swimming records were broken during the 2008 Olympic Games. That is the same year that many top swimmers wore the Speedo LZR swimsuit.

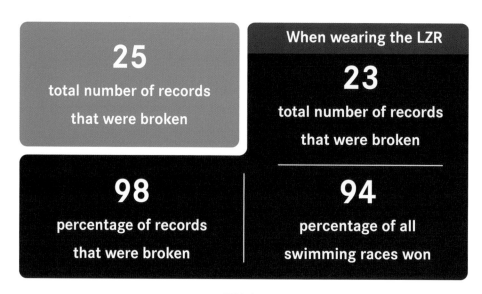

25
total number of records that were broken

When wearing the LZR

23
total number of records that were broken

98
percentage of records that were broken

94
percentage of all swimming races won

2020, Inverse

FASTEST MARATHON

4.5 HOURS
average time it takes to complete a marathon

2 HOURS
considered the shortest amount of time a person needs to complete a marathon

5
percentage of marathon runners who finish in under 3 hours

1 HOUR, 59 MINUTES, 40.2 SECONDS
Eluid Kipchoge's record-breaking unofficial marathon time

In 2019, Eluid Kipchoge ran an unofficial race. He broke the 2-hour marathon record. He did it wearing the Nike Air Zoom Alphafly Next 2 shoes. His shoes were made to improve "bounce" and heel-to-toe drop. Bounce is how much a person moves up and down while running.

2019, ABC News

THE ROAR OF THE CROWD

All teams want home field advantage. That is when teams play in their home stadiums. They are more familiar with their field. And they have a lot of fan support. Loud crowds help players feel energetic and ready to win. To increase their home field advantage, some football stadiums are engineered to be extra loud.

In 2013, Seattle Seahawks fans set a record for loudest stadium noise level at 137.6 **decibels.** The Kansas City Chiefs fans broke that record the very next season. They reached 142.2 decibels.

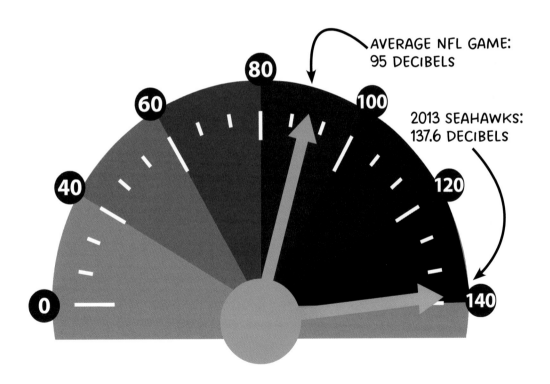

AVERAGE NFL GAME: 95 DECIBELS

2013 SEAHAWKS: 137.6 DECIBELS

0 40 60 80 100 120 140

TOP SIX LOUDEST STADIUMS

The loudest stadiums have features that help make them so loud. Some have walls that are slightly more curved. Some have concrete or metal that helps sound travel better.

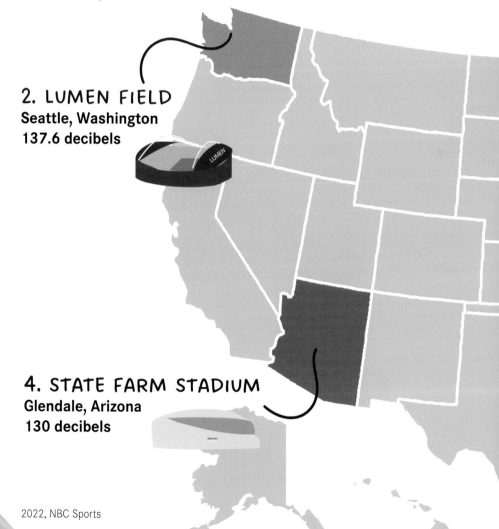

2. LUMEN FIELD
Seattle, Washington
137.6 decibels

4. STATE FARM STADIUM
Glendale, Arizona
130 decibels

2022, NBC Sports

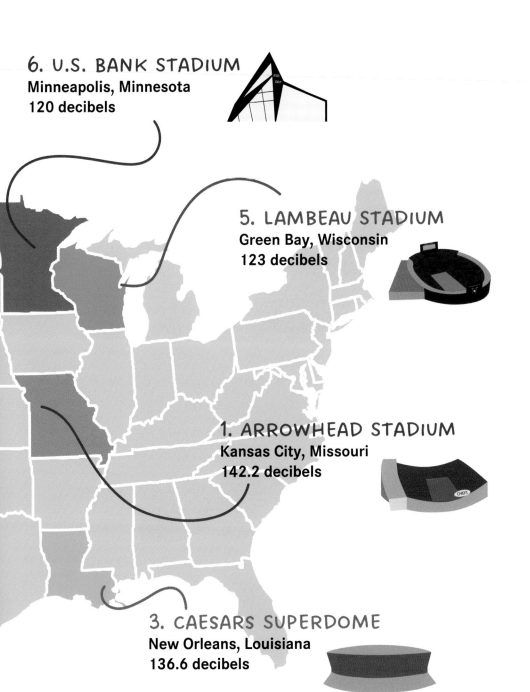

6. U.S. BANK STADIUM
Minneapolis, Minnesota
120 decibels

5. LAMBEAU STADIUM
Green Bay, Wisconsin
123 decibels

1. ARROWHEAD STADIUM
Kansas City, Missouri
142.2 decibels

3. CAESARS SUPERDOME
New Orleans, Louisiana
136.6 decibels

21

ACTIVITY

Improve a Sport

Now it's your turn to think like an engineer! How will you change the game?

Materials Needed

• Library or internet access   • Poster board   • Markers or crayons

1. Choose a sport you'd like to improve. Do some research on your sport of choice. What equipment is used? What do athletes wear? Where do they play?

2. Come up with an idea of a way to engineer an improvement to one of the aspects of the sport.

3. Sketch out your idea on poster board. Label the parts. Explain how your changes will improve the sport.

4. Present your idea to your class, friends, or family. Ask them if they have suggestions on ways to improve it even more.

FIND OUT MORE

Books

Swanson, Jennifer. *The Secret Science of Sports: The Math, Physics, and Mechanical Engineering Behind Every Grand Slam, Triple Axel, and Penalty Kick.* New York: Black Dog & Leventhal, 2021.

Ventura, Marne. *Learning STEM from Basketball: Why Does a Basketball Bounce? And Other Amazing Answers for Kids!* New York: Sky Pony Press, 2021.

Online Resources to Explore with an Adult

Fun Kids: So What Is Sports Engineering?

Sports Illustrated for Kids: Baseball of Tomorrow: Smarter Equipment

Bibliography

Morrison, Jim. "How Speedo Created a Record-Breaking Swimsuit." Scientific American. 2012

Pare, Dustin. "For Better Health, Safety of Athletes Which Playing Surface Is Best?" Global Sports Matter. 2019.

"The Evolution of Technology in Sports." Hire Intelligence. 2022.

GLOSSARY

acoustics (uh-KOO-stiks) the qualities of a room or space that affect how sound travels through it

calories (KAL-uh-reez) the amount of energy a certain amount of food gives the body

concussion (kuhn-KUH-shun) an injury to the brain from hitting the head too hard

decibels (DEH-suh-bulz) units of measurement used for sound

drag (DRAG) the force of air pushing against an object in motion

engineering (en-juh-NEER-ing) the work of designing and creating new tools, machines, or buildings

innovations (ih-nuh-VAY-shuns) new creations that advance a field of work

league (LEEG) an organized group of sports teams that play against each other

polycarbonate (pah-lee-KAR-buh-nut) a strong type of plastic

shot clock (SHAHT KLAHK) a clock that counts down how long teams or players have to try to score

velocity (vuh-LAH-suh-tee) how quickly an object is moving

INDEX